SHANGHAI ■

1949: **THE END OF AN ERA**

Photographs by Sam Tata

Introduction by Ian McLachlan

B.T. Batsford Ltd · London

Photographs and compilation © Sam Tata 1989
Introduction © Ian McLachlan 1989

First published 1989

ISBN 0 7134 6428 3

Printed in Great Britain by
Bath Press, Bath
for the Publishers
B. T. Batsford Ltd
4, Fitzhardinge Street
London W1H 0AH

Contents

DEDICATION
For Rita, Lydia, Ratna, my
brother Jehangir and Henri C-B, witnesses to
history and the end of an era

A NOTE ON SAM TATA

Born in Shanghai in 1911, Tata has been a photographer since 1936. A fortunate meeting with Henri Cartier-Bresson in 1948 in Bombay and the subsequent close and lasting friendship resulted in a complete break with traditional photography. He returned to Shanghai in 1949, and recorded events before and after the advent and establishment of Mao-Tse-Tung's government in China. He emigrated to Canada in 1956, since when he has been published in four books, and has had numerous exhibitions; his photographs are included in many major collections, such as the National Portrait Gallery, London.

A NOTE ON IAN McLACHLAN

A writer, teacher and curator, Ian McLachlan has published two novels, co-written three plays, and has published poems and short stories, translation poems and short stories, translations and critical articles in magazines and journals in Europe, Asia and North America. He is, inter alia, Professor of Cultural Studies at Trent University, Canada.

THE FALL OF SHANGHAI *IAN McLACHLAN*

Shanghai was the greatest colonial city the world has ever known, but when it fell, nothing happened.

The fall of Shanghai, the liberation of Shanghai: hardly any of the people I've talked to about it, no matter what side of the rhetorical fence they come from, remember anything significant at all. In the first place there was so little to remember. But then, beyond that, there's a feeling somehow of shame that such a symbolic moment should have passed by with so little drama.

Throughout the spring of 1949, the Kuomintang government had boasted of turning the city into a new Stalingrad; Shanghai would never be lost without a heroic and bloody struggle.

Beneath all the talk, however, the sense of unreality grew. Chiang Kai-shek announced his retirement, then came to Shanghai to declare: "Shanghai will fight to the end." A few days later, he withdrew abruptly to Taiwan. At the same time, the vaults of the Bank of China were secretly emptied of their stocks of bullion and the entire gold reserves of the country were spirited after him. The President had pulled off the biggest bank robbery of all time.

For their part, the Communists didn't seem to be in any hurry to take Shanghai. Slowly, one of their armies circled round to cut it off from the south as the city waited fearfully.

Rumours and panic spread. Most of the rich Chinese and some of the Europeans fled by any means possible: with shiploads of rice and cotton, planeloads of gold, truckloads of jewellery and tobacco, till Shanghai was stripped bare.

Thousands of the poor were caught up in the rush. They had nothing to gain by fleeing, and probably they didn't even know why they were doing it. But they crowded into the train stations, and if they couldn't squeeze into the carriages, they climbed on top. Many of them were swept off by the first bridges they came to.

Everybody else waited in paralysed anticipation. And then, in a single night – 25/26 May 1949 – history passed them by.

Sam Tata went to bed early. "Some time after midnight, I heard machine-gun fire. Lying there, I said to myself, what does one do now? Does one roll off the bed and crawl under it? And I thought, oh, the hell with it, and the firing stopped and I went to sleep. The next morning, I woke up and it was all over."

That same day, he took a photograph of three Chinese businessmen – Kuomintang sympathizers till that moment, surely – standing on a sidewalk reading newspapers to find out what had happened.

Their city had rolled over with hardly a whimper. And what would they ever be able to say about it?

It's not surprising that a child's memories are the most vivid. Jind Singh is a respected Indian journalist now, but at the time he was the shy, curious son of a struggling Sikh farmer. They owned a small stable of cows that supplied milk for the Europeans.

"My parents told me not to go out on my own," he recalls. Everything was very confused. There was a curfew and you could hear firing on the other side of the city. We all knew it was only a matter of time before the Communists came in.

"At the intersection on the road where we lived there were half a dozen Kuomintang troops who had very little to do. They were sitting idly and they were restless. They got up and started firing at a bakery. The owner came out and pleaded with them and gave them some biscuits. Then they raided a bicycle shop and they were riding round and round on the bicycles shooting their guns in the air. That was all the activity we saw.

"There was a Kuomintang barracks on the other side of the lane behind our compound and occasionally they would fire at anybody moving down the lane. The night before the Communists were expected to come in, people decided to set up a fire-fighting committee. Each household was required to supply two buckets of water and one member who would stand on guard. They were supposed to wear black if possible. My family all took shelter on the ground floor of the stables. I couldn't sleep with the cows moving about, and one of my friends lived out on the road. So I crept over to his place to watch from the verandah. But there was very little happening."

Jind Singh pauses and looks at me with a grin. "Actually, there was quite a lot happening. You see, my friend's father had been caught in the curfew and he couldn't get home. So his mother's boyfriend had come over to be with her. They were in bed together and when I went through the bedroom to go out on the verandah, they were a bit embarrassed and tried to stop what they were doing. But after I had gone past a couple of times they said, 'Just go straight through,' and they didn't take any notice at all of me after that. Really, everything was so quiet outside, I think we spent more time looking in from the verandah than looking out.

"I was still there in the morning when the first few Communist troops walked in and ordered the Kuomintang soldiers to surrender. About half of them put their hands up while the others started firing. The Communists returned the fire and within five minutes it was all over, at least in that area. The Communists just moved the bodies to one side and covered them with their uniforms. People came running out of their houses to offer them hot water and noodles. They declined everything except for the water; they wouldn't even accept the noodles. That was my first impression of the Communists."

Long before that day, Shanghai was a city of the blind. When people talk to me about it – and how they all want to talk! – their words shimmer with rich memories. But it is always gossip, the surface of their lives; never the whole picture, never a sense of what might have been happening underneath.

I keep nagging away at them with the same questions.

"What about the poverty?" I ask Freddy Elias, the old stockbroker. "Didn't it become unbearable after a while?"

I'm thinking of the trucks that used to prowl the streets of the International Settlement on a cold winter's morning. Their job was to pick up the bodies of the poor who had died of exposure or malnutrition during the night.

Freddy Elias blinks at me in puzzlement. He lived all his life in Shanghai before the Communists forced him to leave. For him it is still quite clear: "Shanghai was the most wonderful place in the world. You could really live there."

Now he is in his eighties, his tall frame slightly stooped, but the vigour, the grasping enthusiasm for the simple material world are undiminished. Every morning he comes into his office in Hong Kong, surrounded by blaring phones and the noise of Chinese brokers arguing, joking, gossiping at the tops of their voices. Two of them stand in the doorway waiting to take him to lunch.

"Poverty?" he says impatiently. "No, no, it didn't worry us at all. The stock market stayed open right up till December, 1941 when the war broke out. Before that we had our troubles, local troubles. A few of the chaps were a bit hard up after the big smash in 1929. But nothing to worry about. There was no poverty. Business went on as usual. Shanghai was a wonderful place for recovery, you know."

Why did you never see what was really going on? I want to ask as he holds out a limp, dismissive hand.

"Did none of them ever see what was happending?" I say to an old American woman who went there first as a tourist in 1938. She sits in a small apartment in Kowloon with three locks on the grille outside her bolted door, surrounded by the garish fragments of Ching dynasty silk embroidery that she has spent her life collecting.

She tells me to turn off the tape-recorder while she thinks about it. Then she says hesitantly: "The poverty was underneath the surface. The poor were kept off the main streets. But still you couldn't help seeing it in the rickshaw boys. If you were at all conscious, at all observant, you had to see their shoulders, how emaciated they were. And yet people who lived there would be completely oblivious to it. They wouldn't even see the boy; they'd just sit in a rickshaw."

Solly Bard, the doctor, was one of the few whose curiosity forced him to see. Of course, he wasn't born in Shanghai either. He arrived there in 1932, a boy of sixteen on his own, full of the idealism that had been instilled in him at the Russian school in Harbin. "I had ideas, I mean to say, we all had in those days, and my ideas have not basically changed. My views have always been socialist. I can't see another fair way of dealing with people."

He leans back in the armchair in his clinic. He's about to retire; finally, it will leave him with more time for chess, his violin, archaeology, all the other passions of his life. Unlike so many others, he wasn't drawn to Shanghai as the Paris of the East it was reputed to be. He went there for one reason only — to learn enough English to get into the medical school in Hong Kong. But what he found himself in the middle of was a world that was horrifyingly alien to the cultured, thoughtful milieu he had left behind in Harbin, the doomed Russian city in the middle of Manchuria. The Shanghai Public School where he enrolled was an exact replica of an English boarding school with its first elevens and second elevens, its Officers' Training Corps, its scouts and its prefects. He smiles scornfully: "I thought it was all perfectly silly and immature."

At weekends and on holidays he used to go out on his bicycle and ride around the Chinese working-class areas of the city. "The Europeans never went there. They were completely unaware of what was happening. On the surface, the International Settlement was well enough run. From the administrative point of view it seemed to work well: the streets were clean; the lights came on at the right time, that sort of thing. And on the positive side, there was a fair amount of culture. There was the symphony orchestra and the museum. There was the opera. That way it was all right.

"But the atmosphere was dominated by the club life." (I remember Sammy Tuttleman, another ex-Shanghai Public School boy, saying to me: "If you didn't have a club, you weren't alive.") "There were these terrible cliques of people who were very well off and spent most of their time at the club or the race course, not caring at all what went on around them. There was certainly hardly any contact with the Chinese, except the wealthy ones, and I believe the wealthy Chinese didn't have much contact with the poor Chinese, either."

His voice grows hard and he smacks the palm of his hand on the desk. "Beneath it all there was rot and corruption; an immense amount of sweated labour. I have seen shops where children were working sixteen hours a day, for food only. That was Shanghai in the thirties. There was incredible poverty, and in fact there were two quite separate systems of justice. It was common knowledge that if a drunk foreigner ran over a Chinese, he could simply pay $400 on the spot, and that would be that."

He pauses for a moment, then tries to make sure I understand. "You see, it was a reflection not only of the terrible system that the Europeans had brought with them, but also of the desperate views which the poor Chinese had of life. They knew they couldn't get justice, so they might as well take $400. Whichever way you looked at it, there was complete indifference: a glitter and glamour on the one side, and on the other, just. . .just nothing."

In the evenings, to make some extra money, and probably out of adolescent fascination too, Solly Bard played his fiddle in one of the many Russian cabarets. "I was only allowed to play from eight to ten. Some of the dance hostesses really took to me, a youngster of sixteen and probably quite cute. They used to make sure I left at 10 before things. . . well, before they really got going. I played the dinner music and afterwards they would all come over. 'Off you go, back and do your homework.' But even then I could see all this glitter and wealth. . . ."

He stops and shakes his head, over fifty years later and still full of anger at the memory. "Oh, I thought Shanghai was a rotten place, rotten to the core."

The memories are always so intense. Whether they are good or bad, whether Shanghai was a place you loved or whether it filled you with impotent rage, it stamped the most vivid images on your life.

What gave it this power to survive, if only as a mine of incompatible symbols?

"It was a city of contrasts," everybody ends up telling me whenever I ask them.

Well, yes, of course. But isn't that just one of those catch-phrases we hang on to, not so much to define the real contradictions in our existence as to keep them comfortably at a distance?

Every city is a city of contrasts, after all.

I switch the tapes back and forth till the voices mix in my memory.

J.R. Jones, the Druidic poet and self-styled scholar of Etruscan and Sanskrit and Buddhist culture, friend of Lloyd George and Paderewski, was 'J.R.' to everyone in the Far East long, long before *Dallas*. As secretary of the Municipal Council of the International Settlement from 1927 to 1940 he was the effective ruler of Shanghai. He talks about how it was "the most cosmopolitan city in the world, the kind of city that probably never existed before and certainly never will again. We had a professional orchestra of over a hundred, mainly from the Scala in Milan and the Conservatoire in Petrograd. Shanghai was the place where, if you wanted culture you could get it aplenty; if you wanted sin, you could get it too."

The voice drones slowly on as he talks of secret diplomatic missions and army intelligence, and then at the end of the interview he tries to sum up the meaning of his life: "Insofar as I have any philosophy, I've lived as fully as I can and taken advantage of all the opportunities that life offered, especially in the way of adventure." But the voice on the tape is hollow and dead. And J.R. Jones, who lived so long death seemed to have overlooked him, is dead now, too.

As is Billie Liddell who went to Paris every year with a Russian maid to buy the latest fashions, who danced all night with the Duke of Kent at the Café de Paris and went back with him for breakfast at Buckingham Palace. Billie Liddell who went up to nomadic Mongolian villages with a Russian trainer to select her own ponies for the race tracks in Shanghai. Her life was lived for gambling and horses and parties: "I used to gamble, gamble, gamble, oh, till four or five in the morning, go home, have a bath, get into your jodhpurs, go down to the race course and ride my ponies. I must say, life was pretty good in Shanghai." But there's no dancing in the voice on the tape; it's slurred and covered with calluses.

I listen to Lawrence Kadoorie, one of the richest men in Hong Kong, and therefore, in the world. He talks about how his father left Baghdad to work for the Sassoons in the opium trade in China, about Marble Hall, the family mansion in Shanghai, "lit by no less that 3600 electric bulbs in the ballroom alone," where Rabindranath Tagore, Margaret Sanger and the Panchen Lama visited them. "The Panchen Lama arrived complete with his own orchestra which, in addition to numerous drums and cymbals, included two twelve-foot-long trumpets. The horns of these trumpets were held by bearers whilst the players blew from the other end. At the reception given by my father on that occasion, this orchestra, together with Shanghai's leading jazz band conducted by Whitey Smith, occupied rival positions on the stage, and I can assure you it was an evening well worth remembering.

"Shanghai," he sums it up, "was a place where one could dance all night, go riding at six o'clock in the morning, work all day and yet not feel tired."

But there's no joy, nor even nostalgia, as he talks; he presents his memories like a report to an annual general meeting.

What these "contrasts" leave me with in the end is not the vitalizing tension between work and play. Nor is it, in social terms, the fundamental interdependence of wealth and oppression. What stays with me, long after the tapes are silent, is the eerie contrast between the grasping, materialistic life that's asserted and the horrible deadness of the voices.

It was a city without a history.

Shanghai had never been one of the great cities of China. There was nothing there that anyone needed. For centuries it survived as a small port on the yellow mudflats at the estuary of the Yangtze River. It attracted no attention until 1842 when Britain claimed some of the swampy land just to the north of the walled Chinese town as part of the settlement of the war which had been fought to impose the opium trade on China.

The foreign concessions were staked out in the mosquito-infested triangle between the Huangpu River and the Soochow Creek. Warehouses and, later on, increasingly grandiose banks and hotels were built along the edge of the river (the Bund), and as the population grew, the concessions expanded into the interior as well. They developed their own independent administrations and insisted stridently on separate courts and legal rights for foreigners.

There is no 'history' of the International Settlement in Shanghai. There is only an endless seepage of gossip.

In a sense, all modern cities are colonial cities. Wherever they are situated, they prey on their hinterland, sucking its life and destroying its values. Of that kind of city Shanghai is the archetype. The archetype because it reached perfection as no other colonial city ever did. In other colonies the white man's burden implied responsibility as well as power, no matter how narrow or hypocritical the expression of that responsibility might have been. There were always order, morality, faith to be brought to the uncivilized darkness — futile attempts to counterbalance the guilt for the exploitation and oppression.

Shanghai was responsible to nothing other than itself and its own prosperity. China, after all, was not, had never been, a colony. The European traders didn't find themselves shackled to a whole complex system of authority. They didn't have to bother about the kind of rambling, far-flung administrative structure that sapped so much of their energy in India. They had no obligations of conscience, no debts to pay.

Shanghai grew rich as China disintegrated in the early years of this century. The country's breakdown fueled the city's prosperity.

Hardly anyone in Shanghai knew or cared what was happening in China. China was an exotic land where J.R. Jones could visit his Buddhist monasteries or Billie Liddell raced ponies across the Mongolian steppes. Outside, at the very edges of the city, there was a whole continent of instability, famine and suffering, but it might as well have been an undiscovered planet. The confusions and extremism of Chinese politics merely served to endorse the well-oiled machinery of international business.

Everything was done to keep the chaos at a safe distance.

"Did Chinese politics have any impact on the life of Shanghai?" I ask Freddy Elias.

"Not to any great extent," he replies. "We had the Municipal Council which was run by very capable men, and we had a wonderful police force — a big Chinese force but all the officers were British. And we had our own volunteer corps. I was attached to the volunteer intelligence department because I spoke Chinese. I used to drive around with these chaps, seeing various spots where there was supposed to be trouble. There was quite a lot of excitement but we got through it all right. Nobody worried very much."

If, by accident, the outside world did penetrate the city's close confines, it was in the form of schoolboy adventure tinged with absurdity.

"We had a friend who was a warlord," Eric Cumine, the Eurasian architect, tells me. "A sort of warlord failed. He lost, and he ran into the International Settlement to hide. He stayed with us for nine months in the attic. A warlord in the attic," he grins. "So many of these chaps used to hide in the International Settlement. It was the only place they wouldn't be tackled."

Who could take that kind of politics seriously?

And yet China's chaos was vital to Shanghai. The refugees who were driven to the outskirts of the city by war and hunger and exorbitant money-lenders provided an endless supply of indiscriminate labour for the new textile factories. Shanghai, whose initial wealth had been dependent on the European enforcement of the opium trade, now was about to go one step further: its ever increasing prosperity was based on a whole culture's total collapse.

Nobody bothered to imagine that out of that collapse a new direction for China might be defined. Or that this new China might turn on the old Shanghai, wonderful and rotten city that it was, and wipe it out completely.

The tide of Chinese history would not leave Shanghai untouched forever, after all.

The Chinese in Shanghai never quite knew if they belonged there or not. They had to be unchallengeably wealthy not to feel the least bit insecure.

Like Joseph Hsia, the banker.

I lean over the tape-recorder trying to make out his heavily accented Shanghainese voice above the noise of the air-conditioner in his office. From time to time he bursts into high-pitched giggles as he tells me about his childhood. "I think we have around forty servants. In our mansion we have three tennis courts — everything just like a king. It cannot compare with other Chinese. We are — how you say? — top notch."

Strangely, the one aspect of the family house he doesn't tell me about is the one which should have been most memorable. It's one of his friends, another banker, who taps me on the wrist after a fifth or sixth double Rémy Martin. "You know Joe Hsia?" he whispers. I nod. "His family was so bloody rich they had their own gold smelter in the back of the house."

But Joseph Hsia prides himself on being very philosophical. "During that time we must have bodyguards. My uncle was kidnap by gangsters. After that I have two bodyguards myself — one Russian, one Chinese, one keeps an eye on the other? — wherever I go. When I go to school even, they sit there in the classroom with me. They learn more than me," he laughs. "When you are young, you know, and you have a very easy life, you don't learn nothing. Only I have learned from the Russian bodyguard. I went to his quarters. We pay him $75 per month and lots of tips from some of the guests. I learn from this Russian bodyguard, they have a big castle – no, a palace – back in Russia before the Communists kick them out. They have eight white horses to pull their carriage; really, a palace, you know. So then I realize, some day Joseph Hsia will be just same like these Russian bodyguards."

Not that the realization made life any the more insecure for him. I ask him if he ever came across any anti-Chinese feeling in Shanghai, the city where some of the benches in one of the parks had tasteful little plaques on them saying: NO DOGS OR CHINESE ALLOWED.

"No," he insists, "there was no anti-Chinese feeling among foreigners. They just have feelings against the inferior classes, the ordinary Chinese who were same like slaves. All these foreigners, they make lots of money out of China; why they be anti-Chinese?"

For many Chinese, however, wealth was no guarantee of stability. It might help them to skim lightly across the troubled currents of a racist society. But it produced a deeper cultural insecurity that led to a debilitating over-refinement. Take the case of John Wu, the factory owner. For him it was not money that Shanghai signified – money was simply taken for granted; it was pleasure and the obsessive pursuit of beauty.

"I have been to more parties than anybody else in the whole world," he tells me with a sigh.

We sit drinking all through the night in his apartment till dawn comes up across the window and his stories overflow with pathos. "My mother was very young, much younger than my father. I think when they got married she was sixteen, the daughter of a big merchant, really rich, owns a couple of ships, that sort of thing. So when he died, mother being very young and there was no son, they want somebody dependable, a good businessman, for a son-in-law. That's how they choose my father; he was already a friend of the family."

John Wu strokes the 'mutton fat' glaze on a piece of Ming blue and white porcelain. "My mother wasn't like my father at all. She liked the house to be full of people, her friends and her playmates, bankers, doctors, diplomats, government officials, people who liked a good time, you know, hangers-on. Sometimes they would come after dinner, fifteen or twenty of them, uninvited, and the servants had to start cooking again. It made my father so angry. One Sunday morning they already start arriving, my father came in and kick them all out, just tell them, get out of the house. That produced a lot of tension.

"I was afraid of both of them.

"My father was very hot-tempered. Every morning this fellow prepares his shirts and ties and socks, that sort of thing. If it was not properly prepared he'd get mad and punch him. And my mother, I wasn't too close to her, either. When we went past her door, we have to tiptoe. Any noise and she is aroused, we'd get a spanking. She would get up at lunchtime and then her hairdresser comes every day. Then she practise her sword-fighting and later in the afternoon there were rehearsals for Peking opera. She was a very keen actress. That was all she did: act and play."

Beautiful women became the sole reason for John Wu's being. "We had this maid, she was eighteen, used to carry me around. And one day she sort of undress herself, bare her chest. I thought it was quite beautiful, looking at her breasts, so I remember I start sucking at her. Imagine, a kid five years old. Afterwards she took me out and buy me ice-cream. Later on she became a dance hostess."

As we talk, a little pekinese yaps in the corridor. Then the door of the room squeaks open an inch or two and he catches a glimpse of his wife crouching there, listening to his confessions. The stories become more outrageous.

He tells me about the sing-song girls of Shanghai, his ideal of the feminine. "You have to understand, there was nothing exploitative about the relationship with them," he insists. "It was pure aestheticism. The highest-type girls, it was never a question of buying sex. You give them presents, maybe get them to organize a dinner or something, give them a present for doing that. It wasn't a question of going to bed with them. Maybe you wait six months; if they like you, at last they would. If not, they keep on saying no. But you don't regret anything, even then, because the possibility of being successful in the end was enough, enough pleasure in itself. They were very intelligent women, very cultured, trained to please, not like these Hong Kong housewives." Giggling, he glances trowards the door and it slams shut. "If anybody make it clear he expect something in return, it just show he's a cheapskate."

Later on, John Wu weeps as he describes how, when he was already in his mid-twenties, his father locked him up to prevent him from living with the one woman he ever loved. She married someone else. And later still, when we are both drunk and maudlin, he breaks down again as he tells me about the young English official in the Hong Kong Trade Department who's refusing to give him the export licenses he needs unless he pays a bribe that will force him, into bankruptcy.

The racism of Shanghai was no mere accident. On the contrary, it was the cement that bound the whole precarious life of the city together. It provided an unstable society with a hierarchical sense of cultural security. There was always somebody else to be despised: the Chinese by the English; the Indians and Eurasians by both; the Sikh policeman by the businessman; the Chinese coolie by the Sikh.

Almost everyone, when I first ask about it, denies that it even existed.

Freddy Elias, for instance, boasts of how he flouted the old prejudices. "There wasn't much mixing in the early days. We did a good business with them, mind you. But I think I can tell you that I was the first one to dance with a Chinese girl in public in Shanghai. Everybody just sat and gaped at us and said, 'My God!'

"This poor girl – she was a beautiful girl; she was married and she was so nervous she was trembling. I said, 'Don't be silly, they'll get used to it, it's a matter of time.' All my friends said, 'My goodness, you're certainly brave. Aren't you afraid what people will think?' And I said, 'Listen, you'll all be doing this a year from now.'

"That was 1923 or '24. And a year from then all of them were dancing with Chinese girls. Oh yes, they were beautiful dancers all right, made the best partners, no doubt about it."

For rich young men like Joseph Hsia or John Wu, racism was such a marginal factor that it could easily be ignored. Money provided the perfect insulation. But you only had to move a step or two down the social ladder to find a completely different viewpoint.

K.P. Cheong, the reporter, comes from a typically conservative middle-class family. Almost all his life has been spent working for foreigners. He started out with an English-language newspaper in Shanghai and since then, in a variety of different capacities, has served the diverging causes of the American and Taiwan press with equal assiduity.

On the surface, he is dapper and polite, full of helpful facts about Chinese history. His daughter brings us tea and he sits back comfortably in the big armchair. But when I push him a little the wrong way, the bitterness begins to show through. "Yes, there was some fraternization between Chinese and English, but very little. We tried to organize a P.E.N. Club.

There were a few Europeans who were interested. Emily Hahn, for instance, an American woman, very Bohemian. She was living with a Chinese dramatist and they both enjoyed several pipes of opium. She went around with a cigarette holder out to here and a monkey on her shoulder. But that kind of contact in the end was very tenuous. The only people who professed any concern for the Chinese were the missionaries. They came to save our souls and eventually found the Chinamen had no chance of redemption."

K.P. smiles briefly behind his glasses, sips some more tea and then goes on passionately: "If you walked into the Hong Kong and Shanghai bank, you had two sections, one for foreigners, one for Chinese. Even though your section might be crowded like hell and the other section was deserted, you could never go over to that side.

"For most people it was worse than it was for me. The rickshaw boys, for instance, were treated very rudely: 'Chop, chop,' a kick on the bottom, 'run faster, run faster.' Or too good, on the other hand: 'I've made you carry me on the rickshaw, maybe I should carry you' – that's just as bad, just as insulting.

"Let me give you an interesting example." And then K.P. Cheong launches into a story that is so glib and polished he has obviously told it many times before.

"I was in a rickshaw," he says, "and we stopped at a red light. Well, rickshaws had a way of wiggling through, and the rickshaw made a left turn, but a car came and cut in. The rickshaw boy had to brake very quickly and the foreign driver stopped and started shouting and a Sikh policeman came rushing over.

"I said, 'What's wrong?' The foreigner said the rickshaw scratched his fender. 'Oh,' I said, 'that's very bad, but tell me, which part of the rickshaw scratched your fender?' He said, 'The axle.' I said, 'Which scratch are you referring to?' He said, 'Right here.' Big scratch, serious damage.

"I said, 'Just a minute.' I got out a piece of string and I measured the axle against the scratch mark. 'Impossible!' He said, 'Maybe his fender scratched mine.' I said, 'Which part?' He said, 'How do I know?' I said, 'All right, I'll measure the front part and the back part. . . . Impossible!'

"He said, 'Oh, I'm sorry, I made a mistake.' I said, 'Don't apologize to me. You have to say sorry to the rickshaw boy. Now. Here's a policeman. Do you want to go to the police station?' He said, 'No, no, no, no need.' I said, 'Well, then, please apologize to the rickshaw boy.' He said, 'I'll pay him $2.' So I spoke in Chinese to the rickshaw boy and said, 'Are you satisfied?' He said, 'Without you, I'd be in trouble.'

"So the foreigner paid him $2 and the rickshaw boy took me home. He tried not to let me pay the fare. I said, 'He paid you what you had a right to. He wasn't paying my fare.' But he said, 'You protected me. You gave me face and I'm happy with that.'"

As I watch the fixed mask that covers K.P. Cheong's anger almost perfectly, I can see how a lifetime of subservience to the foreigners might have produced this self-righteous fantasy as a form of impotent compensation. I don't believe his story for a second, and he catches the flicker of disbelief in my expression. For one exposed moment the hatred flares in his eyes yet again. .

For most of the Chinese who lived on the outer fringes of the International Settlement, the experience of racial humiliation would have been a kind of luxury. For the vast, exploited majority the colour of the person who was doing the exploiting didn't really matter all that much.

In that sense, the experience of racism was finally just one more way in which the consciousness of the middle-class Chinese was deflected from a clear understanding of all that was wrong with the society to which they were desperately clinging.

For Ng Yuen, it was simply irrelevant. After all, he never met a foreigner in all his years in Shanghai.

"Not one?" I ask – a different kind of disbelief. "Not ever?"

"How can I? I am so rich man?" He laughs. "My father, he went away when I am little baby. My mother dead with typhoid. My auntie sell me and my brother to a factory boss. She say, 'You are apprentice now.' All I do is work fourteen, fifteen hours a day. Seven days a week. Just for rice. Bad rice, too."

Ng Yuen is a *pak-pai* (an illegal taxi) driver in Hong Kong. He has a share in his own car now and maybe in two or three others as well. He leaves the present a bit unclear – after all, he has no reason to trust me. But the past speaks for itself. He pulls up at a stall that sells the large flat Shanghainese rice noodles that we both like and we get out. He's a fat shiny man with receding hair, wearing baggy brown shorts and a white singlet. He perches easily on a small stool and I squat awkwardly beside him.

"When I was sixteen my brother get killed. Only fifteen, nice boy, very clever, more clever than me. The machine in the factory catch his arm and cut it off. Right off. All his side cut, too, right down here." He touches his smooth, plump thigh. "He's screaming, I'm screaming. But we get him out of the machine. He's still alive, still conscious. Outside, the boss had a new car, new leather seats, very nice car. The other workers say, 'You must take him to the hospital.' But the boss say, 'No, he make my seats dirty.' All the workers very angry, but the boss don't change his mind, just shout, 'Back to work, back to work.'

"I took my brother to the hospital in a wheelbarrow, but he's dead already."

I swallow my noodles in silence. "What kind of car?" I ask dully.

"Vauxhall, real lousy car." Ng Yuen goes on smiling in the humid sun.

The camera sees what the eye overlooks.

(Does the tape recorder hear what the ear shuts out?)

"Did nobody ever see what was going on?" I kept asking in these interviews.

Sam Tata did. He saw it all through the camera.

His background was not so very different from that of most of the other foreigners I talked to. He went, like them, to the Shanghai Public School. He was educated by expatriate teachers in the values and myths of English middle-class life. In 1926, during the anti-British demonstrations that were organized by the Communists, he was one of the boy scouts who delivered mail in the effort to break the postal workers' strike.

When he left school he went to work for his father "as a kind of glorified clerk" in the family business. They managed two textile mills and speculated in cotton on the international market. But his heart was never in the work; whenever there was a chance, he would slip out to the bookstore around the corner. He read detective stories and Flecker and Rupert Brooke. "My dad was indulgent. He despaired about me, poor man, till the day he died."

Sam lived with his parents and brothers till after he was forty. "Who would want to rebel and leave a house so full of servants? What was there to rebel against?" It was, as he came to see it later, "a hothouse existence. I thought everybody in the world lived like that".

When I first met him I asked him my stock question about the poverty. His answer was more humane than Freddy Elias's, but no less accepting: "We looked at it with different eyes. If you let the poverty get to you, you might as well have left Shanghai. There was no solution to it. So you built up a kind of armour against it."

There's nothing in any of that to explain how these photographs happened.

When Sam Tata started to take pictures of the chaos and conflict in the streets of Shanghai in the spring of 1949, it was the camera that made him see, and start to understand, what was going on.

On the obvious, initial level there was the sheer excitement of getting involved. The camera allowed you to do things you wouldn't otherwise have been able to do. It was the key to dangerous adventure.

Listen to him talking about the photographs he took of the trial of some Communists by a Kuomintang military court:

"I was passing the police headquarters and noticed all the commotion around the entrance. I saw a Chinese photographer I knew and asked him, 'What's happening?'

"He said they were waiting for the trial of some Communists who'd been caught by the authorities. So I asked him, 'Can I get in as your assistant?'

"He persuaded a guard at the gate to let both of us in. Once we were in the courtyard, we ran up some stairs to one of the balconies. There were two tiers of balconies, all of them full of people looking down and waiting for the accused to arrive. We had to wait for an hour or so. I kept taking light meter readings because it was beginning to get dark and I was worried about there not being enough light.

"Then a truck came in with these three chaps and they were pushed out.

"I took some shots of the start of the trial from the balcony, and then a photographer from *Life* got permission to go down into the courtyard. I followed him and got right in behind one of the accused. He had a placard with his crimes written on it tied behind him and a soldier was pulling his head back by the hair. I was kneeling down with the camera up to my eye when one of the guards turned around. I found myself looking straight into the barrel of his gun. His finger was on the trigger. I suppose the safety-catch was on – there was no reason for his taking it off, but you never know. It didn't bother me too much at the time. I just ducked under the barrel, stood up and went on taking photographs.

"Much later on that night, it hit me and I thought, 'My God!' Of course, there was no real danger, but you never knew what might happen.

"The whole trial was just like a nightmare. The conclusion was foregone from the very beginning. At the end the accused were made to eat a last bowl of noodles and taken away to be executed."

The camera's viewpoint is never simply that of the detached and indiscriminate observer. It is never neutral. It frees the photographer from the normal social routines of his life. And it creates a space between him and what he sees. Not an emptiness; a space in which a critical sense of relationships can be established.

(Can I say the same for the tape-recorder? In many ways, yes. Once the initial awkwardness is over, it frees the one who talks from the usual constraint; the microphone requires no debt of guilt. And the one who listens, later, in his own time and context, hears differently too. A more focused hearing, not blurred by this gesture or that grimace; a critical placing. I wouldn't have caught the deadness in those voices, as they talked of the wonderful life of Shanghai, if the tape-recorder hadn't pointed it out.)

As far as Sam Tata was concerned, the camera enabled him — perhaps forced him — to draw on the buried, inactive parts of himself. There was, for instance, the compassionate humanitarianism his Parsee father had always drummed into him: the need to treat all other human beings with charity and respect. Those may be dangerously ineffective abstractions when one is rich and everybody else is invisibly poor. But there is nothing abstract in these photographs.

Look at the picture of the woman begging from the wealthy Chinese businessman. He sits there in his rickshaw with his oiled hair, his *cheong-sam*, his fashionable western shoes, and he refuses to acknowledge her. But by doing so, he also refuses to acknowledge the camera. He turns it into an enemy, too; an enemy with a long memory. The camera sides with the beggar-woman and with the rickshaw boy who looks questioningly straight towards it.

It is always like that. Though Sam Tata may have been rich himself, though he may have ridden in many rickshaws, the camera forced him to take the part of the poor.

There's another suppressed aspect of Sam Tata's life that the camera brought to the surface. Whenever I've asked him, he has always insisted that he never suffered from the racism of Shanghai. Certainly, his life was well cushioned against it. But it must always have been lurking there. As an Indian, there were places he couldn't go, things he couldn't do. It didn't matter to him very much, and all of his conditioning must have taught him to suppress any potential anger or resistance.

But in the photographs of the celebrations on Bastille Day at the French Club or the one taken a little later at the swimming pool in the grounds of the race course, it emerges again in the form of a harsh, satirical mockery.

He is not one of these people. His sympathies are elsewhere. Through the camera, he sees them quite differently from the stateless refugees waiting, waiting for their exit visas, or the man carefully sweeping up every grain of spilt rice in the street.

The camera is not just a mechanical tool. It becomes the crucial instrument in a process of moral self-definition.

As we look at these photographs, we share in that process too.

"How did you know when the People's Liberation Army would finally move in?" I ask Mak Lai-heung, the Communist journalist. I'm expecting some tale of the underground – secret messages, at least. After all, he was sent to Shanghai, disguised as a gold dealer, to cover the Liberation of the city.

"It was when the Kuomintang decided to hold a victory parade." He grins at the puzzlement on my face. We sit by the window in his apartment as torrents of rain gush down outside. From time to time his daughters clack across the wooden floor on clogs. I hear them again on the tape, and somewhere birds I didn't notice then are singing.

"It had become a ritual for the Kuomintang," he explains. "Whenever they started to flee from a place they would stage a victory parade. This was the strangest parade I've ever seen. Just a long line of army trucks flying different coloured flags and streamers, with signs saying, "Celebrate the Great Victory." There was no-one except for the drivers. All the trucks were empty. Then I knew it was all over and the Kuomintang was down to its last minutes. That evening I got a phone call from a friend of mine who was a reporter. He said, 'The boss is leaving.' I knew what he meant."

But even then he missed the actual moment. "We listened to the radio to find out what was going on. There was only music. I remember it was Beethoven's Ninth. Usually, the radio stopped broadcasting at midnight, but that night it just went on and on. By two there was still nothing happening, so we switched it off and went to bed. The next morning I ventured out into the street and I saw Liberation Army men sleeping right there at the entrance to our lane. I went over and talked to one of them who was awake. I said, 'When did you get here?' He said, 'One o'clock in the morning.' We were still listening to the radio at that time and they were already outside. They made no noise at all."

It's my turn to smile. "News should always be so easy," I say.

As his wife brings in the dishes she has cooked for lunch, he describes the Kuomintang stragglers who roamed the streets, dumping their American carbines in the gutters and going into people's houses, not to rob, but to beg for civilian clothes. "They didn't dare to cause any trouble," he says with gentle contempt. "They knew everyone was against them."

"The transition was perfectly organized," he goes on as we move to the table. "In fact, Shanghai wasn't really taken over by the Liberation Army. It was taken over by the workers who were in the city already. There had always been a strong underground network of Communists within the trade union movement. Before Liberation they had already organized themselves into various groups. There was the Factory and Property Protection Squad to resist any possible Kuomintang sabotage. And the police posts were all manned by workers. They had the armbands ready in advance.

"Everything happened so smoothly. There was no need for a curfew, even on that first night."

Mak Lai-heung sits back for a moment in obvious satisfaction, a sincere man, completely at ease with his image of the past.

★　　　★　　　★

Is that, I ask myself, the point at which it all ends?

The collapse of one mythology, the start of another?

It would be simplest, certainly, to leave it at that, with the ideological assurance that seemed at one time to be so nearly true.

But there's another story yet, as there always is.

On the other side of the flat ideology is a knot of personal trauma.

The nightmare of Marion Peng.

She was a young Scots girl who married a Chinese doctor in Edinburgh in the autumn of 1948. He threatened to kill himself if she didn't, but already on the boat out to China at the end of the year she discovered that he was still married to someone else. As he walked down the gangway after they docked in Shanghai, he told her to walk behind him and carry his case.

He deserted her almost immediately. "I used to go around the dancehalls and the cabarets looking for my husband. All I can remember is the painted faces of the girls. They always seemed to be laughing at me. I kept on saying, 'I'm Dr. Peng's wife and I'm looking for him.' I went all through those places. When I remember it, it's as if I can hear screams in the background."

She's a middle-aged woman now, with an elegant house looking down across the beautiful, polluted harbour of Hong Kong. Her voice is high and lilting, moving easily into laughter or tears.

Why did he marry her in the first place?

"I suppose it gave him face to have brought back a British wife. But at the same time it didn't fit in with the plan of things. He didn't share any of what was wrong with me. I had to absorb all the hurt myself. Before he came to Scotland he'd been in love with a girl in Hunan, a nurse who committed suicide because he couldn't marry her. I think he was still in the middle of that trauma in Edinburgh when he threatened to commit suicide himself. It was all very confused, very unhealthy. I had no way of understanding all these things, and even now I don't."

What, I ask, did she mean by 'the plan of things?'

His commitment to the Communist Party!

She didn't find out about it till she was in hospital at the time of the Liberation. She was having a baby and a nervous breakdown simultaneously.

"There was some fighting around the hospital, but I can't remember being afraid.

"I do remember the wounded soldiers lying all around the wards and all along the corridors, and the place with the heat and the stench and everything was terrible. They were Communist soldiers and Nationalists, too, I think, all in the same place. We were told a general was coming to visit the wounded soldiers. A general for me was lots of gold braid, but they said, 'There's the general,' and he was wearing a worn dirty uniform and canvas shoes.

"I was in a ward opposite the labour room. You could hear all the noises from there and one of the nurses came out laughing and said, 'Oh, they just pulled the head off the baby of that mother who's been screaming.' I couldn't stand it any more, and I was left all alone. My husband wasn't there; he said he was off dancing.

"Later, I tried to find out how he fitted into the whole thing. I knew there were political meetings going on all the time, and the nurses were always being called away for them. I never even knew he was a Communist until suddenly he took over as director of the hospital. From what I understood, he had made a trumped-up political charge against the very nice man who had run the place before.

"All the nurses were talking about freedom. They were going to work with each other to fulfil their own destiny. They said this was the first time in their history that the ordinary people had a chance to determine the future of their own country. Of course, when I look back on it, they were right. But for my part, I was too sick, too mentally sick, to have any idea of anything apart from survival. And the obsession with finding a way out."

Now that it is all over, what does the term 'Liberation' mean in the context of a city like Shanghai? It's a catch-phrase now in the official histories, consecrated by its capital 'L'. In its use a deliberate choice, an emphasis, has been made. The word 'revolution' would imply the rising of one class against another, a victory and a corresponding defeat. 'Liberation', the word suggests, was a whole country joining together against an alien, exploitative system; it was the expulsion of a corrupt government that had been sustained only by foreign intervention.

Yet the Communists, for all their precise rhetoric, knew well enough that those alien values had deep and widespread roots in the artificial soil of Shanghai.

They moved very cautiously to eliminate them.

They even waited six weeks before holding the first big parade to celebrate the Liberation of the city.

As he pokes into his mouth with a toothpick, Mak Lai-heung solemnly explains why it took so long. "We had a lot of discussions, you see. We didn't want to offend anybody. You have to understand, we couldn't allow it to seem like a 'victory' parade. Shanghai had not been conquered; it had been freed."

The parade that was finally held was meant to keep everyone happy. There were the bright costumes, the gongs, the streamers, the dragon dances of all traditional Chinese celebrations. There were floats organized by local trade union groups bearing propaganda slogans and political cartoons or gigantic portraits of Mao Tse-tung and Chu Teh, the Commander of the People's Liberation Army. And in the center, there were the P.L.A. soldiers themselves, more than a quarter of a million of them walking silently on felt slippers, with their captured American rifles and machine-guns. They brought their prizes too – the most impressive display of power that the people of Shanghai had seen in a century of foreign rule: an hour-long procession of modern tanks, armoured cars and field artillery, all of them new and American and freshly painted with big red stars.

As night fell, it began to rain but the parade went on by torchlight. The distinction between marchers and spectators blurred. Everyone was chanting the slogans on the banners – "Let's Take Chiang Kai-shek Alive", "Develop Production", "Support the Sino-Soviet Alliance", "Down with Foreign Imperialism" – as they swarmed along the great avenues, Edward

VII and Joffre, of what had once been the foreign concessions.

A new city began to grow in the carcass of the old.

On the surface, the changes might have seemed to be very gradual. There was still Scotch in the store windows and Ronald Reagan's films went on playing in the cinemas; beggar children still ran after ladies in brocade *cheong-sams,* threatening to smear their dresses with filthy fingers if they didn't get a hand-out.

But at every level, the quality of life was affected by the values of the new regime. No detail was too trivial to be overlooked.

"Did the Liberation make any difference to you?" I ask Jind Singh.

"No, not really," he shakes his head. "I was just a child." But then, with a smile, he remembers. "Oh yes, at school, of course. Things changed very quickly. It was a Catholic school, St Francis Xavier, run by Marist brothers. Every week the principal used to come into assembly and read the reports and, if somebody hadn't done his work properly, he would be caned in front of the whole class. The Communists put a stop to that right away. 'No more caning,' they said. You can imagine how happy we all were with them after that."

One memory releases a flood. "And on the street-cars the conductors became much more courteous, too. They began shouting the names of every intersection, and when a corner was coming up they would warn people to hold on tight. Campaigns were introduced to clean up the lanes or to stamp out vermin and insects. Anybody who caught twenty flies was given a towel as a prize. . . ."

Above all, inflation, the major problem of China since the end of the Japanese war, was dealt with simply and directly. In the last days of the Kuomintang administration, the spiral had intensified to a point at which it was an adantage to be paid in the morning rather than the afternoon. Individual survival came to depend increasingly on an elaborate network of barter totally divorced from the completely useless currency. But the Communists clamped down on the speculation that had spurred inflation. The silver coinage which had undermined the value of paper money was made illegal. Wages were pegged to the price of rice, and the hoarding of rice was banned.

"That was the biggest problem of all, actually," says Mak Lai-heung. "The merchants had been used to buying a shipment of rice and then keeping it in their warehouses to drive the price up. First of all, we called each of them in and asked them to co-operate. It was all very polite. Some of them did, but most went away thinking: 'These Communists, they're really soft, they don't know what business is all about.' But then they found a couple of weeks later that a whole network of state stores was being set up. They couldn't manipulate the market any longer. They had to get in line or go bankrupt."

★   ★   ★

Only the foreigners were by-passed.

They, whose well-being had been the whole city's *raison d'être*, found themselves suddenly on its margins. Many of them had stayed on in the hope that after a brief upheaval life would return to what they called normal. After all, the city couldn't run without them; business would have to go on.

But they were wrong, uncomprehendingly wrong. It became more and more difficult for them to operate in the same old ways, and official compliance could no longer be bought. So they found themselves going back again and again to government offices, waiting for exit visas. There was a little inconvenience and a lot of grumbling, but for the most part their daily routines changed very little. They swam, took tiffin; the parties in the clubs were more raucous than ever. For many, it was the longest period of leisure in their lives and they look back on it with frustration and bitterness.

But not Prince Gigo.

Why, it's hard to say. After all, he was one of the riffraff the Communists threw in jail.

He's a White Russian, a Georgian, from Harbin. Igor is his real name and much of his life has been lived on the fringes of one underworld or another. As a young man he worked for Tu Yueh-sun, the gangster who had a secret alliance with Chiang Kai-shek, and he tells me lurid stories of gang-wars and factory-sized brothels, of a crazy plot to assassinate the Bishop of Shanghai and blame it on the Japanese. Now, with his fading romantic charm, he has found work as an actor, playing stereotyped heavy roles in dozens of the third-rate movies that are always being made in Hong Kong. As we walk together through the nightclub area of Kowloon, the children and a lot of the bar-girls wave to us. "Prince Gigo," they call after him, affectionately, mockingly, "Gigo, Gigo."

Later, sitting over tea and gin in the ornate lounge of the Peninsula Hotel, he talks with a puzzled respect for the Communists.

"Why did they put you in jail?" I ask.

He won't say directly, just hints at spying, though it was probably the black-market, and maybe sleazier business, too.

"But they treated me well, correctly," he insists. "We were allowed one ounce of oil a month and we always got it. How they fed us so well on the small amount of money they had, I'll never know."

He bites into another cream cake and groans about his waist line. "What impressed me most was the chairs."

I look at him blankly.

"The prison I was in," he explains, "was the one where the Kuomintang had kept the Communists to interrogate them, and you could see from the chairs how they had resisted. There were these special chairs in some of the cells; they didn't use them on me, they didn't have to. The chairs were nailed down and there were bars across the waist to hold the prisoner in. But some of the nails were almost pulled out of the floor and the bars were all bent. You could just imagine how hard they fought to get at the men who were interrogating them."

A frown crosses Gigo's face and he shakes his head to get rid of the image. In the background, brightly uniformed bell-hops are descending on a group of tourists who have just driven in from the airport in the Peninsula's fleet of Rolls Royces. Gigo looks them over carefully and the puzzling memory floats away.

No revolution can be made up only of victory parades and gentle social reforms. Or even of heroic martyrs, for that matter.

"It seemed as if life was one long meeting in the early fifties," says Mr So. "Just one meeting after another. A lot of people found it hard to adjust. They said, 'We don't have enough time for our own lives any longer.'" He smiles, "But they said it very quietly."

Mr So was a waiter in the Shanghai Club before the revolution; now he's the manager of a state-owned store. The ideological struggles of the past thirty years – the Great Leap Forward, the Cultural Revolution, the trials of the Gang of Four – have raged around him without deflecting him. He still listens to his classical records (Brahms and Schubert are his favourites) and he still reads the thoughts of Chairman Mao, though they are no longer fashionable.

"There have been times – the early fifties was one of them – when people who want to interfere in everyone's life had too much influence. How do you call them in English? Nosy parkers?" He laughs with pleasure at an old fluency. "They would go around snooping, trying to spy on other people. They thought they were better than anybody else, so they ought to have power.

"There were all these meetings. Some of them were useful; they told us what was happening, how our lives could be changed. But there were the public confession sessions as well. Somebody who had committed sins in the past would stand up and say, 'I have done this and that,' and he or she would bow in front of the people. If the crime was serious, he would be taken to a labour camp; if it wasn't he would just be reprimanded and that would be that. A lot of people confessed to things they hadn't really done. It was accepted as a new way of life.

"Later on, during the Korean war, the campaigns against capitalists and bad elements among the workers became much more. . . fierce. The authorities were arresting so many people, they didn't have enough jeeps or police vehicles to haul them in, so they used buses to go around and take them to the police stations or the prisons.

"One day, I saw a group of workers going to a factory whose owner had had a very bad reputation. They dragged him out into the street and made him squat on his knees with his hands behind his head. People read out his crimes and pointed fingers at him. Later, I heard he killed himself.

"That was a time when a lot of rich people committed suicide. They usually did it by jumping out of upper-floor windows. There was this joke: don't walk on the sidewalk, you might get hit by falling bodies."

★　　　★　　　★

Through it all, the city changed completely.

The old Shanghai had been totally cut off from the country around it. Or if there was a link, it was that of the tumour to the body it attacks. Now the life of the surrounding land runs in and through the city.

Everyone knows what it means to work in the factories and the agricultural communes. The beggars and prostitutes and pickpockets have gone from the Nanking Road. The brothels and the clubs have been closed and the racetrack houses a scientific library. The financial heart of the city has lost its importance. The traffic jams of shiny American cars with their screeching brakes, all pressing into the downtown area, have given way to trucks of produce and millions of bicycles, all trying to go in different directions. The pace of life has lost some of its frenzy. People don't seem to run everywhere at a constant trot any longer. There is time, occasionally, to stroll, through the endless maze of lanes and alleyways. Time to sit in the corner store where you can fill your flask or kettle with hot water, and talk about what's happening, and what isn't.

Shanghai, the great colonial city, is now the largest village in the world.

EXPLANATORY NOTES AND REFERENCES

BUND An embankment; an embanked quay. The Shanghai Bund – the city's skyline. It once included the Shanghai Club, the Customs House, the Hong Kong & Shanghai Bank, the Palace Hotel, the Cathay Hotel and the British Consulate among other buildings.

CHIANG KAI-SHEK (1887-1975) Statesman and general. After assuming power in 1928, he converted the Kuomintang from a party dominated largely by Kwangtung leaders to an organ responsive to him. His stern and stubborn personality became the symbol of republican China. President of the Executive Yuan, equivalent to the position of Prime Minister, from December 1935 to 1945 and President of the Republic from 1943 till 1948. Chiang fled to Taiwan in 1949.

CHU-TEH (1886-1975) Commander-in-Chief of the Red Army for many years, he became associated with Mao Tse-tung in 1928 when their forces combined to form the Fourth Red Army and to establish the central communist base in Kiangsi. From 1950 to 1959 Chu served as Vice-Chairman of the Peking government.

THE CHINESE COMMUNIST PARTY Founded in 1921. At the First Congress in Shanghai in July of that year the total membership was less than 60, amongst them the rising star Mao Tse-tung.

CHOU EN-LAI The leading international spokesman for the People's Republic of China, served as Foreign Minister. However, he was best known within China as the Prime Minister in the Central People's Government. He retained the respect of virtually all factions and interest groups through to the Cultural Revolution. However, from 1974 up until his death in 1976 he earned the enmity of the 'gang of four' and suffered sustained political attacks. He did however leave behind him a reputation almost equal to that of Mao himself.

INTERNATIONAL SETTLEMENT Created in 1863 by the merger of the British and American zones, hitherto separated by the Soochow Creek, its affairs were run by an elected body called the Shanghai Municipal Council.

KUOMINTANG (KMT) The Nationalist Party. Its origins go b ack to 1905 and Dr Sun Yat-sen who in 1921 became its first President. By 1927 Chiang Kai-shek had installed his own Nationalist Government in Nanking, making it the capital of China.

LIBERATION On 25 May 1949 Shanghai in its turn was formally liberated by the disciplined Red Army known as the People's Liberation Army (PLA).

MAO TSE-TUNG (1893-1976) Leader of the Chinese Communist Party and founder of the People's Republic of China. An aesthete, tall and pale, with long sensitive hands, he was nonetheless stubborn and there was a steel rod of pride and determination that ran through his personality. Edgar Snow said of him: "The influence of Mao Tse-tung throughout the Communist world of China is probably greater than that of anyone else."

GENERAL MARSHALL General George C. Marshall was sent by President Truman to China at the end of World War Two to assist in the uninfication of post-war China by democratic means. He did his utmost to bridge the gap between the Nationalists and the Communists but all his efforts ended in failure: he left China in early January 1947.

OPIUM WARS In the early nineteenth century American, Portuguese and British traders were freely smuggling opium into China as 'currency' (instead of hard silver) against tea, silk and other merchandise from that country. The British were heavily involved – the East India Company being among the heavyweights. There were violent protests from the Emperor and a series of incidents broke out, finally leading to war. A defeated China in 1842 was forced to open up five ports as treaty ports and eventually cede Hong Kong to Great Britain.

PEOPLES LIBERATION ARMY see LIBERATION

SOO-CHOW CREEK Now called Suzhou Creek, it is a tributary of the Huangpu River which flanks the Shanghai Bund.

TAIWAN see CHIANG KAI-SHEK

YANGTSE RIVER Also known as the Yangtse-kiang, it is the fourth longest river in the world at 3200 miles. The Whangpoo is a tributary of this great river.

REFERENCES: *Red Star Over China* by Edgar Snow (1978, revised edition); *Chinese Looking Glass* by Dennis Bloodworth (1967); *China* by Harry Schwartz (1965); *When Tigers Fight* by Dick Wilson (1983); *In Search of Old Shanghai* by Pan Ling (1983); *The Chinese Revolution* by Tibor Mende (1961).

SHANGHAI

1949: *THE END OF AN ERA*

1 Early May: Kuomintang guard post on the Bund

2 Traffic jam on the Szechuan Road, early May

3 China Travel Service, early May: crowd milling around, hoping for railway tickets

4 North Station, Shanghai, before April: Kuomintang officers with refugees leaving the city for Hangchow

*5   Family on the move: boy in the
basket awaits his parents amidst goods
and chattels*

*6   Nationalist soldier in third class
carriage to Hangchow, April*

7 *The city viewed westward from the Broadway (now Shanghai) Mansions overlooking Soo-Chow Creek, before May 1949*

8 A Communist is brought to trial by Nationalists in early May. . .

9   . . . and after being condemned in company with a fellow Communist . . .

10   . . . is then taken by truck to his execution

11   *Kuomintang soldiers flee Shanghai on 24 May, the day before the liberation by the Red Army*

12   *Crippled Kuomintang soldier left behind expresses his plight with characters chalked on the pavement*

13 *The Yang-ko peasant dance
performed by a People's Liberation Army
theatrical group*

14   Propaganda cartoon showing a People's Liberation Army soldier about to bayonet Chiang Kai-shek (part of 4 July Cultural Parade)

15   Beggar boy

16 Beggar uses sidewalk for his tale of many troubles

17 *Worker's parade on Nanking Road*
(one of Shanghai's main streets)

18 Tableau enacted during a parade in summer

19 *July: Liberation Parade in Nanking*
Road

20 *People's Liberation Army marching in Liberation Parade in Nanking Road, July*

21 *Cultural Parade, 4 July: a Chinese worker breaks his chains*

(

*22 Posters of Mao Tse-tung and Chu-teh,
Cultural Parade, 4 July*

23 *14 July: Bastille Day at the French Club*

24 *July/August: swimming pool in the Race Course grounds at the International Settlement*

25 *Bastille Day at the French Club*

26 *Young foreign refugee*
waiting to embark on the Wooster Victory

27 *Before May: Europeans waiting to leave Shanghai*

28 *Nuns leaving Shanghai before May from Shanghai & Hongkew Wharf No. 5*

29 *Pavement display of old* LIFE *magazines for sale*

30 *Magazines being hawked
outside a curio shop*

31   *Old men outside a clock shop*

32   Beggar woman

33   *Man collecting spilt rice*

34   *Beggar boy having a hurried
lunch*

35 *Street urchin begging from two fastidious young women*

36 *Lux advertisement with actress
Greer Garson*

37 *Pedicab drivers at a street corner*

38 *Man and child asleep in a doorway*

39 *Child at play in a bamboo stroller*

40 *Peasant woman with a pipe*
outside a boutique

41 Beggar boys at play on the steps of a bank

42   *Cages with song birds*

43   *Travelling children's library*

107

44 *Old sewing amahs outside a hat shop*

45 *July/ August: poster-seller*

46 *Street vendor outside the Capitol Cinema*

47   *Young woman begs from a haughty*
young man

48 *Summer street quarrel – the younger man has usurped the elder's usual spot*

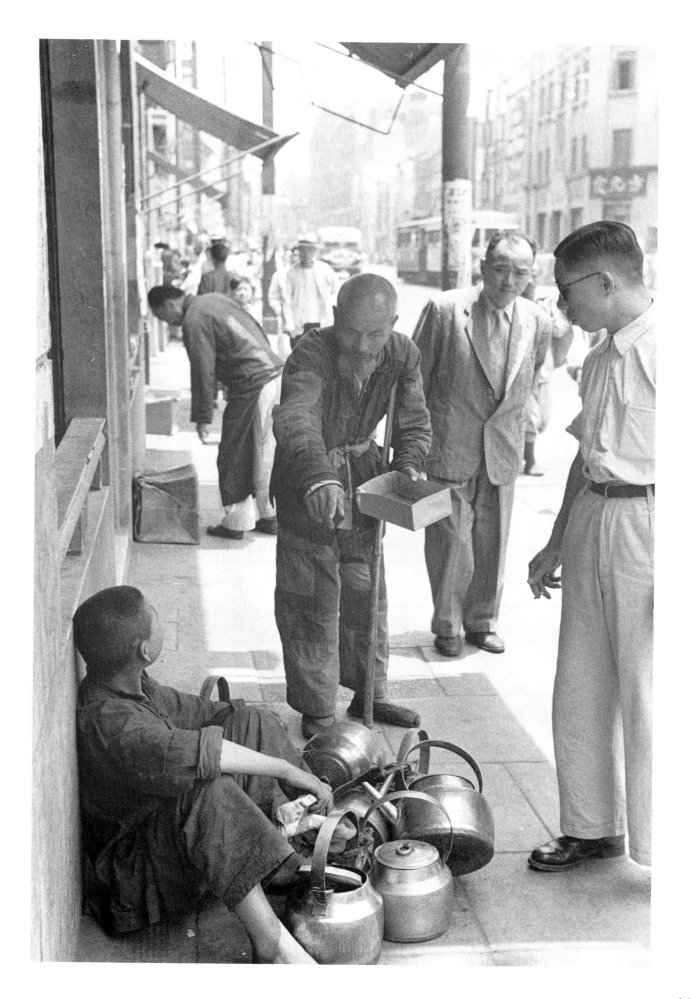

49 *"Photographic reproductions" of Marshall and Mao made with Chinese inks and brush, Nantao, Shanghai*

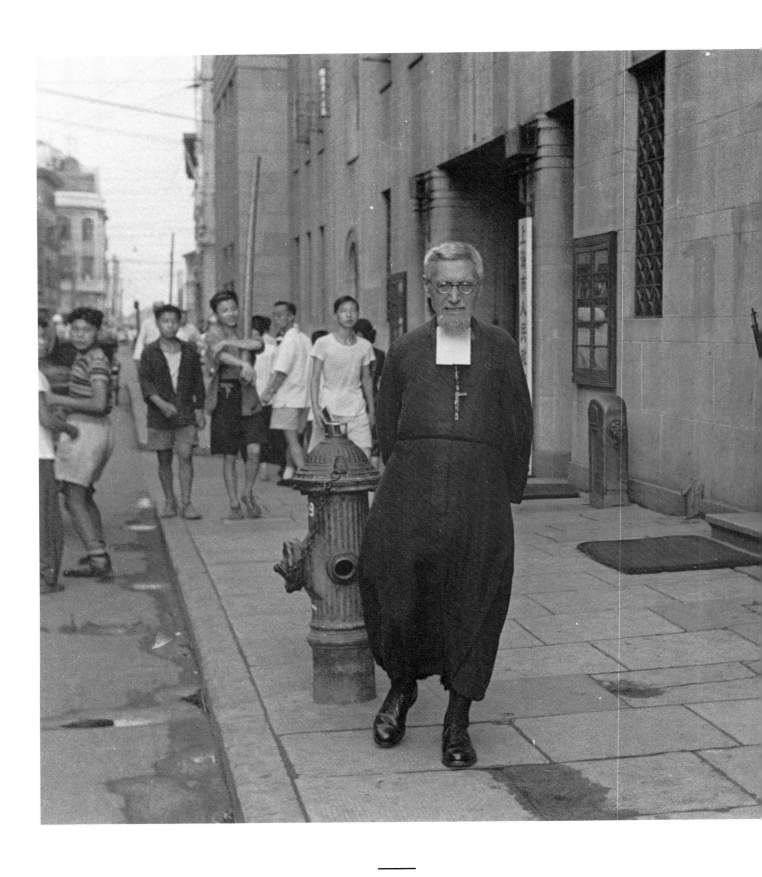

50 *July/August: Catholic priest waiting to apply for an exit visa*

51 *Russian Orthodox nun at the International Relief Organization Centre*

52 *Workers marching in Liberation*
Parade, July

53 *Parade with men on stilts escorting a poster of Mao-Tse-Tung in August or September*

54 *Parade with posters of Chuh-Te,*
Mao, Stalin and Lenin

55 *Blind beggar with spectators at*
Liberation Parade

56 *Soldiers of the People's Liberation Army march down the Bund*

57   *August/ September: spectators at*
a parade

58 *Posters of Mao, Chuh-Teh and Sun-Yat-Sen outside the Shanghai Race Course grounds*

59 *Dragon dance during autumn*

60 *Group participating in a
day-long parade in summer*

61 *Children's parade*

62 *Woman soldiers on parade in
August or September*

63 *People's Liberation Army wife*
and child